EQUAL

PARTS

And Other Poems

Richard Norrid Fletcher

Wayfare Of The Heart Press

Equal Parts And Other Poems
All Rights Reserved.
Copyright © 2016 Richard Norrid Fletcher
v3.0 r1.1

The opinions expressed in this manuscript are solely the opinions of the author and do not represent the opinions or thoughts of the publisher. The author has represented and warranted full ownership and/or legal right to publish all the materials in this book.

This book may not be reproduced, transmitted, or stored in whole or in part by any means, including graphic, electronic, or mechanical without the express written consent of the publisher except in the case of brief quotations embodied in critical articles and reviews.

Paperback ISBN: 978-0-578-18639-9
Hardback ISBN: 978-0-578-18640-5

Cover art and all illustrations by Dona Davies © 2016 Richard Norrid Fletcher. All rights reserved - used with permission.

Wayfare of the Heart Press

PRINTED IN THE UNITED STATES OF AMERICA

In memory of:

Ara A. Golmon
(1915-2009)

Jayne R. Smith
(1932-2011)

Michael Philip Serkess
(1953-1989)

Bret Fulmer
(1960-2014)

My maternal grandmother,
Mary Elizabeth Norrid
(1884-1968)

Contents

n2spin 1

The Runner. 3

Brother 5

Myself, As Two 8

Passing 11

Clarity 13

An Empty Room 15

Who He Is. 16

The Picnic 17

Little Words 19

Teach Me. 20

Stroke 22

Rock Rose 24

Shelter 25

Hunger 28

Poppies 29

Love, Tru. 31

Devon 33

Equal Parts 37

Acknowledgements 39

About The Author 40

About The Artist 40

Have patience with everything that remains unsolved in your heart. Try to love the questions themselves, like locked rooms and like books written in a foreign language. Do not now look for the answers. They cannot now be given to you because you could not live them. It is a question of experiencing everything. At present you need to live the question. Perhaps you will gradually, without even noticing it, find yourself experiencing the answer, some distant day.

Rainer Maria Rilke

Letters To A Young Poet

n2spin

40mins n2spin
Im loozzd
frm my bod-ee
whn I find
thh frame Im
on thh rd up2
Wai mea
leven mls
uphill n2a
scarrd lanscape
ahed
ridrrs
blk helmutz
blk suitz
mplacable siilnt
xcpt 4 chains
thh rttle n grind
reelentlesslee
upwrd
a blk
deth
behin me
rd fallzs a way
n2 nfinit blu
legs numb
heart spin
ning
myselves dis
solving

n2
atmos phere
I Will Not Submit
I Will Not Relent
I Dare U God
r whoevr u r
2 take Me
Now

The Runner

This isn't how I imagined him,
But this is how he came to me –
In a dream, chiseled out of stone,
His heart, hidden, within a heart,

We are running, in tandem,
Two or three strides ahead of me,
For miles now, and I focus
On the small of his back,

My feet follow his,
Our labored breathing
Synchronous,
Just stay with him,

I tell myself, just stay
With the wanting that is
His flesh and blood,
His waist, his thighs,

The harmony
In his chest,
The scent
Of his sweat,

He's testing me!
He tries to pull away, but
I'm on his ass,
He looks over his shoulder,

And I glimpse his eyes
For the first time,
Suddenly, I see what he sees,
He smiles and laughs,

"Catch me!"
And I run faster, and
He slows down, and the
Heart within our heart is found.

Brother

I know you're here
When I feel the weight descend,
The heaviness,
Like a stone within a stone,
Blood runs red over rock,
Heart pounding,
Ears ringing,
Body shaking,
And then,
A shallow pool opens
To receive
A shared
Life's
Stillness.

It is an old wound,
The broken bones of a
A birth and a death,
I have always known you,
But I have never known you,
Never known, until now,

The strength of a stone,
Immovable,
A heart that knows no ending,
The deep well of tenderness
That holds my head above
The water,

Living, breathing,
I am myself, but more,
I am the life you gave for me,
The child reaching for our father,
Only to discover
Your face in the place where
He once stood,
Upon the sacrificial stone,
In a holiness of blood and water,
Mingled,
Where I fell,
And found you,
With me.

Myself, As Two

In the cleft of a hill,
On the edge of a canyon,
In the flow of a river,
Among trees,
And a daylight moon,
Myself, as two,
Where I am the other, and
You are the brother,

And the dream is the draw
Between this side and that,
Where here is there,
And in is of,
All within a thin
Boundary of love,
The heavens,
Intertwined.

You sit astride Comet,
Barely holding
The reins,
A child,

Descending a path,
Into the earth,
The damp, rich earth,
The sun-soaked earth,
The verdant, soul-filled,
Blood-stained earth,

For you,
I am a layer of heaven
Among layers of earth,
The body you lost, and
The stones you found,
Among the bones
That littered the ground,

But, for me,
Child of my heart,
Longed for messenger of the air,
You are the evanescence
Of the river and the trees,
Brother,
Bringer of light and love,

Release me.

Passing

I wonder,
Would you have done anything differently
Had there been signs in the heavens?
The sky on fire or
The moon blood red,
That night I spent dreaming,
The night you ran screaming,
Chasing a demon with spinning tires,
A man always leaving,
A man who loved a game of chicken,

I tried to count the fence posts,
But even then, at the age of ten,
Six times ten seemed more
Real to me than sixty,
The last number I remember
Before someone opened the door,
And I left you to your love.

Spot chased after us –
I think he tried to save me –
But he died, at the top of the hill,
Rendered, like your heart,
A vivid exclamation mark,
Scattered along the highway,
Amid the remains
Of a '63 Comet and a '66 Fury,

I died, too,
But who was left to notice?
Encased in ice,
As I was,
Frozen,
In love's swift
Passing.

Clarity

One day, your heart will collapse
The confusion of the body into
The moment you fell to the floor,
Saw yourself gasping for breath,
The moment your witness picked you up,
Placed you back on the couch,
The gun your father put to your head
Now aimed at your heart,
The difficult deliverance
Of a part
Of the parts.

In that death,
It is not death that calls to you,
But the prayers of the pieces,
And the graces of grief,
The blessings of trees,
Blackberries by the pond,
The morning he died,
And cows,
Curious about your presence,
In the pastures

You walked
With Ruth and Lizzie,
So long ago.

All that was, is.
All that is, was.

In the distance,
A bluebird,
Sweetly singing,
Can you hear the lilt in his song?
Do you see the arc of his flight?
His rust-colored breast
Such a startling gift
Of the clear morning
Light.

An Empty Room

At the time you chose,
And prompted me to wake,
I stood by your bed,
Seeing, knowing,
Time
Slowing,
Letting you go,
Telling you,
Go.

Now,
An empty room,
Your son, a man,
Conscious of his own
Breathing,
Night slowly
Turning toward light,
All our journeys,
One.

Who He Is

He knows
Who I am
Who quotes
ee cummings
and
Ezra Pound

And wants to tattoo
One of my poems
On his back,
Who writes
His own mystery,

The deep, dark
Yes,
Written in snow,
The deep, dark
Yes
That tells the story,

Different from me,
But the same quiet
Listener
Who pauses
To hear
A
Heart
Beat.

The Picnic

I opened the basket this morning,
Sifted through the poems,
Surprised to find you in so many places,
And then, a letter from you that begins,

"Hold your horses, stop the presses,
and don't have kittens,"
So easy to remember what loving you was like,
Thirty-seven years ago,
My half-life,

It was a sky-dream,
It was a lake, still –
It was a rocket that never landed,
Until it crashed,

A bizarre accident from which
You skipped away, and
I crawled,
Unattended (your word).

In this universe of binary stars and black holes,
I am the one standing, having kittens,
Holding you the only way I know how,
Our Sunday lessons?

You're right, you never listened,
Never heard
My theory on Sylvia and Ted,
Never tasted
My desperate attempt at potato salad,

Nev-er let me touch
Pla-ci-do Do-ming-o,
But that's OK, I tell myself,
I understand now,

How being without you
Has served me,
My own little picnic,
For all it's worth.

Little Words

This is the one who scribes little words,
A puny receiver of
The Cosmic Heard,
Deciphering ampersands,
Or an alphabet,
Like dits and das,
A sign, a signal,
A synchronous squiggle?
Then a phrase of remember,
And a page of forget,
God, help this man
You've strapped
To a board,
And blessed with a curse
To scribe
Little words.

Teach Me

Father,
Teach me the song
Of an oriole on a cool, sunlit morning,
An Ozark spring
That tests my heart
With its lingering chill,

I have so little patience,
But something in this song
Compels me to sit on the stoop
And wait, wrapped in the scent
Of his old flannel shirt,

How do I let him go?
Is this a promise I made to you,
That I would return all I learned of love
Because you allowed me to love?

Slowly, fluttering orange and black,
The orioles descend to the feeder,
Taking delight in the freshly cut fruit,
Singing among the leafy green,

There is no song but love,
Teach me,
There is no song but love,
Father.

Stroke

From where I sit,
What I know is,
You put your back into it,
Let the water unfold,
The stillness broken
By glide and stroke,
I am the rising up and
The laying down,
The movement is deep,
To and away,
From and back,
God,
In me.
From where I sit,
What I know is,
You put your back into it,
Faceless brothers,
One with water,
One with sky,
My heart, my breath,
My arms keep time,
The movement is deep,
To and away,
From and back,
"Let it run!"
God,
In me.

Rock Rose

When I die,
Scatter me 'round
The rock rose,
Its dusty pink
To feed on me,

Its seed,
Scarified by fire,
Which is the
Requisite
Rose,

Which is my
Heart brought back
Into the world

Where I live
In the
Rock,

And die
In the
Rose.

Shelter

Late January,
The trees on the ridge, bare,
Silent witnesses,
In stark relief,
To a blue,
Blue sky,
And a low-slung sun.
Somehow I am standing here,
In front of a barn-like house,
Anchored in rock,
Surrounded by
A forest,
Seemingly absent.
I walk into light
Streaming through clerestory windows,
Elspeth oils the floor,
"It's alright," she says,
"Leave me be, I'm saying my goodbyes,"
And later,
"We didn't know, until now,
That we were all awaiting your arrival."
Stephen hands me the keys, and says,
 "I like to look where I'm going,
Not where I've been. Good luck."
Not where I've been,
Where is that place, I wonder?
As I stand in an empty room
Of gleaming birch and cherry,
Immersed in the scent of lemon oil,

And pray,
In silent stillness,
To winter my reasons,
And take refuge in trees.

∞

Let the fields go fallow,
Let leaves gather where they will,
Let ice break open the marrow,
And snow pile high on the sills,

Let go of what you thought was day,
Let go of what you thought was love,
This dream will find another way,
That in the night is mindful of,

The cold, your stammer, his frozen face,
The absence of shadows, a muttered grace,
Can you feel what you already know?
There is such silence in the snow.

∞

Early morning spring,
Snow gives way to rain,
To sun, to sky,
From every window
The earth overflows
With water and light
That washes my head,
My hands, my grief,
The greening branches,
With a psalm,
A promise, whispered
To fern and columbine,
I wake in a
Poem of wood, rock,
Tree and sky,
Shelter
For a man who loves.

Hunger

The woods waken
To light without shadow,
To snow in every branch,
To chickadee and titmice

Who kindle the silence
With movement and song –
Joy in hunger
This Sunday morning.

I listen for a long time,
Then fill the feeders,
Rapt in a cadence
Of black-white,

Blue-gray,
Movement, stillness,
Warmth, cold,
Softness, solidity,

Mute in song and silence,
Until, I, too,
Begin to whistle,
And join the chorus.

Poppies

Today, I found
Last spring's poppies
In the shed,

The heads dry,
Brimming with tiny seeds,
So I gathered them,

Carefully cracked
The outer shells,
Then emptied the pods,

Overflowing,
Into a glass bowl,
And wondered,

Could love be counted like this?

With my hands,
This offering,
And a prayer

For a rich and
Unexpected gift,
Sown in late summer,

To bloom the following spring,
This is my heart,
Made new.

Love, remember me,
And a field of poppies,
Countless, in the sun.

Love, Tru

For Love
So loved the world,
There was you,

Light, poured into life,
Toes and fingers,
Eyes and ears,

The intricate mystery
Made perfect,
And true,

Welcome to grace,
That has a place
Called, "You,"

And to this cobbled path
Of heart and stone,
Upon which

You have come
To walk, and we,
With you, once again,

To gaze at the moon,
Or fly a kite,
Or sail an ocean

In hemispheres
Of blue,
For Love,

That so loves the world,
And us,
There is you.

Devon

There is a place,
Where the Taw and Torridge
Meet the sea,

Where poets walked,
Where Tarka talked,
And otters dwell

In timeless swells of
Leisurely eternity,
A land of rocks and streams,

A land of bogs and dreams,
A land just right for lingering,
And listening,

What will you find
When you seek
The wisdom of your name?

In Farway,
A churchyard yew,
An ancient tree,

That spoke to me
May speak to you,
Expect the wayfare of the heart,

Said she, the Farway Tree,
That is as near to
Life and love as

Blessed be, can be.
This, little sister,
My meager lesson

In paleogeography,
The landscape
Of your name,

Someday,
You'll come seeking,
A poet or a tree,

You'll need more than a day,
A lifetime, maybe, for
Two Moors Way,

In freezing fog,
Or Tarka's Trail,
In summer's veil,

Or Hollerday Hill,
Where the azure world
Stands still,

Whether lost or found,
In small steps or long,
Purposeful or purposeless,

Walk into the Valley of Rocks,
Where the wind
Whispers your name,

Walk into the Valley of Rocks,
Where time itself
Tells your name,

Walk into the Valley of Rocks,
Where the very ground
You stand upon,

Speaks your name –
Devon,
When you grasp this,

That you are of the stones,
The sea and moor,
You will be a poet of the tor,

You will be the one
You're seeking, you will be
The one you've travelled for.

Equal Parts

Lord,
Grant me a heart
Of equal parts,
Sun, moon,
Self, lover,
Sky, earth,
Friend, brother,
Of landscapes of love,
Mountain, ocean,
Of living in dying,
Tree, flower,
Of gratitude in grief,
River, stream,
In your hands,
Forest, meadow,
I am made whole,
Sunlight, shadow,
The sum of the heart is
Equal parts.

Acknowledgements

Bryan Elwood

Dr. Russell Dunckley

Dona Davies

Trey Bartosh

Naomi and Jim Rosborough

Kittie Vanston

Jim and Irene Elwood

Raymond Trevino, Jr., Martha Morgan, Faye Fulton

Lara and Eric Fors

Angela Acree

Stephen and Elspeth Byers

Hollister Rand

Colin Tipping

Paul F. Henry

Stanley Plumly

Dr. Christine P. Ford

Allen Marsh Ford

Daniel James Coker

Jon D. Rakestraw

My mother and father

My brother –

I know that one day I will understand, and that on some level, I already do.

About The Author

Richard Norrid Fletcher was born in Ringgold, Louisiana, on January 4, 1956. He grew up among the woods and lakes of north Louisiana - he was deeply influenced by life on his grandmother's farm in Red River Parish. In 1969, he moved with his parents to the industrial town of Port Arthur, Texas.

In Port Arthur, amid the tumult of the late '60s and early '70s, his love of poetry was nurtured by two extraordinary teachers, Ara Golmon and Jayne Smith. They introduced him to a world of art and literature, and taught him a new vocabulary, a new way of describing and distilling his life experience. They continued to provide guidance, counsel and friendship to him long after high school.

Three other teachers nurtured his development as a writer during his university days: Capt. Paul F. Henry at the U.S. Air Force Academy, Dr. Christine P. Ford at Northwestern State University of Louisiana, and Stanley Plumly at the University of Houston.

Rich lives, works, writes and walks in the Ozarks of northwestern Arkansas. More about his writing and his life's work can be found at www.trustallowaccept.com.

About The Artist

Dona Davies is an artist and illustrator living in Springfield, Illinois. She frequently explores liturgical art in her creative endeavors, and has designed stained glass windows for numerous churches around the country.

www.ingramcontent.com/pod-product-compliance
Lightning Source LLC
Chambersburg PA
CBHW020024050426
42450CB00005B/626